# ORCAS: KILLER WHALES

by Victor Gentle and Janet Perry

**Gareth Stevens Publishing**
A WORLD ALMANAC EDUCATION GROUP COMPANY

Please visit our web site at: www.garethstevens.com
For a free color catalog describing Gareth Stevens' list of high-quality books and
multimedia programs, call 1-800-542-2595 (USA) or 1-800-461-9120 (Canada).
Gareth Stevens Publishing's Fax: (414) 332-3567.

Library of Congress Cataloging-in-Publication Data

Gentle, Victor.
    Orcas: killer whales / by Victor Gentle and Janet Perry.
        p. cm. — (Whales and dolphins: an imagination library series)
    Includes bibliographical references and index.
    ISBN 0-8368-2883-6 (lib. bdg.)
    1. Killer whale—Juvenile literature. [1. Killer whale. 2. Whales.]
I. Perry, Janet, 1960- II. Title.
    QL737.C432G46    2001
    599.53'6—dc21                                    2001020014

First published in 2001 by
**Gareth Stevens Publishing**
A World Almanac Education Group Company
330 West Olive Street, Suite 100
Milwaukee, WI 53212 USA

Text: Victor Gentle and Janet Perry
Art direction: Karen Knutson
Page layout: Victor Gentle, Janet Perry, Joel Bucaro, and Tammy Gruenewald
Cover design: Joel Bucaro
Series editor: Catherine Gardner
Picture Researcher: Diane Laska-Swanke

Photo credits: Cover © Marilyn Kazmers/Seapics.com; p. 5 Photofest; p. 7 © Ingrid
Visser/Seapics.com; pp. 9, 11, 17, 19 © Michael S. Nolan/Seapics.com; p. 13
© Amos Nachoum/Seapics.com; p. 15 © Ingrid Visser/Seapics.com; p. 21
© Hiroya Minakuchi/Seapics.com; p. 22 Joel Bucaro/© Gareth Stevens, Inc., 2001

Printed in the United States of America

1 2 3 4 5 6 7 8 9 05 04 03 02 01

Front cover: An orca, also known as a killer
whale, shows its teeth in what looks like a great big
smile. Who knows? Perhaps it *is* happy to see you!

# TABLE OF CONTENTS

Words that appear in the glossary are printed in **boldface** type the first time they occur in the text.

# STAR OF THE SILVER SEA

A famous film star lives near a small island off the coast of Iceland.  He has not made a movie for some years.  He probably will not make another.

Now and then, his friends take him for a "walk" in the ocean.  There, he sometimes meets up with a **pod** of orcas, or "killer whales."  He swims and plays with them.  Then, he returns to the island and his friends — who do not want him to come back!  *They* want him to stay with those orcas full time.

He has a mouth full of strong, white teeth, holds his breath under water for 15 minutes, and weighs about 10,000 pounds (4,500 kilograms).  Have you guessed?  His name is Keiko, the star of the 1993 hit movie *Free Willy*.  He is an orca, too.

Keiko, the orca, greets his co-star, Jason James Richter. *Free Willy* is the story of an orca who escapes to the oceans and freedom.  In real life, Keiko remained a captive.

# CAN WE REALLY FREE WILLY?

Keiko was two years old in 1979 when he was captured in the ocean near Iceland. Corporations, some rich folks, and thousands of kids donated more than $15 million to give Keiko a chance to live with his own kind.

In 20 years, Keiko has not "spoken" with orcas or practiced orca behavior. Today, Keiko's own family may not recognize him. What if he cannot act properly or speak "orcan"? Will the wild orcas accept him? We don't know yet.

In the wild, most orcas live in groups, or pods, of 6 to 50. Each pod belongs to a larger group, or **clan**. Orcas from pods in the same clan make similar sounds, so each clan has its own special language.

Orcas in this pod near San Juan Island, Washington, and neighboring pods speak a similar language. The language spoken by Icelandic orcas, like Keiko, is quite different.

# USING ECHOES, ECHOES, ECHOES, ECHOES

Orcas are a noisy bunch, and they are not always just chatting with each other. They also make rapid clicking sounds, then listen for echoes to find food and other objects. That is **echolocation**. With their keen sense of hearing, orcas can figure out where things are. They can often tell *what* things are, too!

In the darkness of the oceans, a talent for clicking plus two good ears may be worth more than a fine pair of eyes. But orcas do have great eyesight. They can see well in the water *and* above the surface.

Orcas sometimes lift their heads into the air for a few seconds to take a look at what's going on above their watery world. That is spyhopping.

"Hey, Mom! Look what I can do!" Here, a young orca spyhops while an adult orca swims close by. Often, a group of orcas spyhop together.

# SNACKING AND SNORTING

Different groups of orcas use different methods to catch the different kinds of food they eat. Some groups work as a team to catch fish, like salmon or herring. They herd the fish together, then take turns eating. Other orcas mainly eat **mammals**, like seals, sea lions, and porpoises. They chase down these larger animals and catch them one by one.

Orcas find their food by sight and hearing. Unlike most animals, orcas have no sense of smell. Their **blowholes** are used only for breathing air.

Orcas breathe air, not water. Like all **cetaceans**, orcas are mammals. And, although orcas are also called killer whales, they are not really whales. They are dolphins.

An orca surfaces in the ocean and blows out after holding its breath for, maybe, 5 to 15 minutes. It will need to take a few breaths before it dives again.

# BRINGING UP BABY

Like all baby mammals, orca **calves** feed on their mother's milk after they are born. They nurse for at least a year. Their mothers do not have another baby for at least two years after **weaning** each **calf**.

Orca pods are close family units. Like humans, orcas mate outside their own family units. Males find females from other pods. Unlike humans, however, they then return to their own pod. There, they baby-sit and teach their nieces and nephews.

In orca **society**, the oldest female is the head of the family. Even after child-bearing age, she is there to help raise the young. She may live as long as 80 years — 20 years more than most males.

An orca mother and her calf swim close to the coast of Norway. Orcas have been seen in coastal waters all over the world and sometimes quite far out to sea.

# FINS, FLIPPERS, AND FLUKES

Like all dolphins, orcas have one **dorsal fin** on their back, a **flipper** on each side, and two flattened **flukes** for a tail.

The dorsal fins of orcas are taller than the dorsal fin of any other dolphin. They can be taller than one-fifth of their body length. Male dorsal fins grow to almost 6 feet (1.8 meters) long. That's more than twice as tall as the dorsal fins on females.

Most dolphins have sickle-shaped flippers. Orcas don't. Their large flippers are oval, like paddles. Orcas use their flippers to twist and turn in the water and to touch each other. Their flukes are so strong that they can catch a Dall's porpoise — the fastest porpoise in the world.

With their powerful flukes, orcas can leap high above the surface of the sea. That's quite an achievement for an animal that weighs a few tons.

# LET'S SEE A PHOTO ID, PLEASE

Scientists can identify individual orcas by their dorsal fins. Each fin has a special shape and size and a unique set of scars and nicks. Most scars and nicks are permanent, though more can get added!

On an orca's back, just behind its dorsal fin, is a gray area called a saddle patch. Each orca's saddle patch has a different shape, position, and special colored markings. It often has scars, too. All these features help identify which orca it is.

Scientists on the west coast of Canada and the United States have photographed and identified hundreds of orcas. Identifying orcas helps scientists track orca family relationships and eating patterns. This teaches us much about how orcas live.

Three orcas show off their fins and saddle patches. The orca named "L47" by scientists leads her daughter, "L83," and another orca, probably "L91."

# KILLING KILLER WHALES

For hundreds of years, many people have admired orcas. Others have feared and hated them. They believed orcas were dangerous, especially to humans, so they called them "killers."

Many fishers believed, and still believe, that orcas take too many of "their" fish. They killed orcas to protect their livelihood. Many orcas captured alive have had scars from bullet wounds.

Some fishing fleets have killed orcas for their meat and oil. Thousands of other orcas were caught as **bycatch** — as the fleets hunted other sea food. Many people worried that orcas might be in danger of **extinction**.

Here, orcas are shot with cameras. Orca hunting has been banned in many areas. Happily, killer whale watching trips have taken the place of killer whale killing trips.

# SAVE THE KILLERS

Keiko and other captive orcas have shown how intelligent and gentle these wonderful creatures are. They have helped change the way we think of orcas. Wild orcas have shown us how they care for their young, use language, and learn new skills.

Orcas do kill seals and sea lions. That may seem frightening. And yet, orcas *have* to be good at killing their food. Their survival depends on it. Orcas do not kill humans for food. In fact, orcas hardly ever threaten us, except to defend themselves.

Most orca hunting has been banned since 1986, but we still threaten the survival of all orcas. The fishing business cuts their food supplies. **Pollution** poisons them. If we want to keep orcas alive, we still have work to do and much to learn.

"Look out, little sea lion! That orca's a-coming to catch you." We may feel sorry for the sea lion pup, but orcas must eat. It's all part of nature's cycle.

# MORE TO READ AND VIEW

**Books (Nonfiction)**    *A Day in the Life of a Marine Biologist.* David Paige (Troll)
*The Hostage.* Theodore Taylor (Dell)
*Killer Whales.* Nancy J. Nielson (Capstone)
*Oceanography.* (Boy Scouts of America)
*Orcas Around Me: My Alaskan Summer.* Deborah Page
  (Albert Whitman)
*Whale Watch.* Ada and Frank Graham (Delacorte)
*Whales and Dolphins* (series). Victor Gentle and Janet Perry
  (Gareth Stevens)

**Books (Fiction)**    *Waiting for the Whales.* Sheryl McFarlane (Philomel)
*Whale Brother.* Barbara Steiner (Walker)

**Videos (Nonfiction)**    *Killer Whales: Wolves of the Sea.* (Warner Home Video)
*The Magnificent Whales.* (Smithsonian)

# ORCA QUICK FACTS

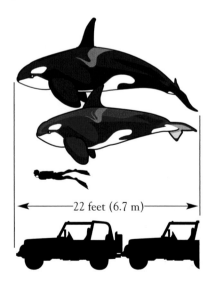

22 feet (6.7 m)

**Average weight of adults**
Females: 6,000 pounds (2,700 kg)
Males:    8,800 pounds (4,000 kg)

**Average length of adults**
Females: 19 feet (5.8 m)
Males:    22 feet (6.7 m)

**Number of teeth**
40 to 52, each about 3 inches (7.6/cm) long

**Length of life**
Females: up to 80 years
Males:    up to 60 years

**Special features**
Orcas are the biggest species of dolphin. An average-sized orca will eat
about 550 pounds (249 kg) of food in a day. They can dive to 100 feet
(30.5 m) below the surface in order to hunt and can swim as fast as
30 miles (48 km/h) per hour in short bursts.

# WEB SITES

If you have your own computer and Internet access, great! If not, most libraries have Internet access. The Internet changes every day, and web sites come and go. We believe the following sites are likely to last and give the best, most appropriate links for readers to find out more about the oceans, whales, and other sea life.

To get started, enter the word "museums" in a general search engine. See if you can find a museum web page that has exhibits on ocean mammals and oceanography. If any of these museums are close to home, you can visit them in person!

**www.ajkids.com**

This is the junior *Ask Jeeves* site — it's a great research tool.

Some questions to try out in *Ask Jeeves Kids*:
- *Where do orcas live?*
- *What do orcas sound like?*

You can also just type words and phrases with "?" at the end, for example:
- *Keiko?*
- *Extinction?*
- *Pollution?*

**www.yahooligans.com**

This is a huge search engine and a great research tool for anything you might want to know. For information on whales, click on <u>Animals</u> under the <u>Science & Nature</u> heading. From the Animals page, you can hear or see whales and dolphins by clicking on <u>Animal Sounds</u> or <u>Animal Pictures</u>.

Or you may want to plug some words into the search engine to see what Yahooligans can find for you. Some words related to Orcas are *whaling*, *red tides*, and *Keiko*.

**www.enchantedlearning.com/**

Go to Zoom School and click on <u>Whale Activities</u> and <u>Whale Dictionary</u> for games, information sheets, and great links for many species of whales, including orcas, bottlenose dolphins, blue whales, sperm whales, right whales, humpback whales, and others.

**www.whaleclub.com**

The *Whale Club* is a great place to go to talk to other whale fans, talk to whale experts, and find out the latest news about all the whales in the world. Find out how Keiko is doing.

**whale.wheelock.edu**

The *WhaleNet* is packed full of the latest whale research information. Some is way cool! Click on the <u>Students</u> and then the <u>WhaleNet Index</u> button to find more buttons and links that will help you find whale videos, hear echolocation, or ask a whale expert a question.

# GLOSSARY

You can find these words on the pages listed. Reading a word in a sentence helps you understand it even better.

**blowhole** (BLOH-hohl) — a hole that whales use for breathing 10

**bycatch** (BYE-kach) — sea creatures caught by accident in nets meant for other fish 18

**calf** (KAF) — a baby whale; plural: **calves** (KAVZ) 12

**cetaceans** (sih-TAY-shuns) — members of a group of sea mammals that includes whales, dolphins, and porpoises 10

**clan** (KLAN) — a group of pods, in which the orcas all speak a similar language 6

**dorsal fin** (DOOR-suhl FIN) — a fin found on the back of most whales 14, 16

**echolocation** (EK-oh-loh-KAY-shun) — the process of sending out and receiving sound to learn about an object or an animal 8

**extinction** (ex-TINK-shun) — the end of life for a whole type of animal 18

**flippers** (FLIP-urs) — a whale's front limbs, like a human's arms or a bird's wings 14

**flukes** (FLOOKS) — the two lobes forming a whale's tail 14

**mammals** (MAM-uhlz) — animals that give birth to live young and feed milk to their young 10, 12

**pod** (PAHD) — a close family group of orcas 4, 6, 12

**pollution** (puh-LOO-shun) — poisons put into or onto the land, air, or water 20

**society** (suh-SYE-uh-tee) — the way that groups of animals (including people) are organized and behave with each other 12

**weaning** (WEE-ning) — the end of the time that mammals feed milk to their young 12

# INDEX